LIGHTNING
BOLT
BOOKS™

Meet a Baby Lemur

Samantha S. Bell

Lerner Publications
Minneapolis

Content Consultants: Dr. Mark C. Andersen, Department of Fish Wildlife and Conservation Ecology, New Mexico State University, and Chris Smith, Duke Lemur Center

Lerner Publications Company
A division of Lerner Publishing Group, Inc.
241 First Avenue North
Minneapolis, MN 55401 USA

For reading levels and more information, look up this title at www.lernerbooks.com.

Library of Congress Cataloging-in-Publication Data

Bell, Samantha, author.
  Meet a baby lemur / Samantha Bell.
      pages cm. — (Lightning Bolt Books. Baby African animals)
    Audience: Ages 5–8.
    Audience: Grades K to 3.
    Includes bibliographical references and index.
    ISBN 978-1-4677-7972-2 (lb : alk. paper) — ISBN 978-1-4677-8365-1 (pb : alk. paper) —
ISBN 978-1-4677-8366-8 (eb pdf)
    1. Lemurs—Infancy—Juvenile literature.
    I. Title.
QL737.P95B45 2015
599.8'3—dc23   2014044316

Manufactured in the United States of America
1 – BP – 7/15/15

Table of Contents

A Big Family

A group of ring-tailed lemurs walks through the forest. It is almost time for the females to give birth!

Lemurs live in groups. Females in the group give birth around the same time.

Many lemur babies are born each year.

The females have been pregnant for more than four months. All the babies in the group will be born in late summer.

Mother lemurs usually have one baby. Baby lemurs weigh around 2.5 ounces (70 grams). That is about as much as fourteen nickels.

Baby lemurs are very small and thin.

A ring-tailed lemur's tail is between 22 and 25 inches (56 and 64 centimeters) long.

Each baby lemur measures about 4 inches (10 cm) long, a little smaller than your hand. Their parents are about 17 inches (43 cm) long. That is the size of a house cat. Their tails are a bit longer than their bodies.

Baby lemurs look a lot like their parents. They have rings on their tails and black masks covering their faces.

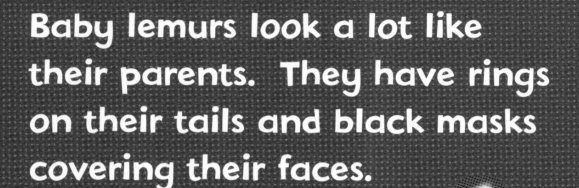

Baby lemurs may be smaller than their parents, but they look very similar.

Groups of lemurs are called troops. **The females in a troop are related. They are mothers, daughters, aunts, and sisters. One female leads the troop.**

Between six and thirty lemurs belong to a troop.

Riding with Mom

Newborn lemurs cling to their mothers' bellies. They crawl onto their mothers' backs after they are a few weeks old. At three weeks old, lemurs also start walking and climbing.

Very young lemurs ride on their mothers' bellies.

A mother lemur grooms and feeds her baby. But she does not work alone.

Female lemurs help take care of one another's babies.

Many baby lemurs come back to their mothers only to eat or sleep. Others are more shy. They hang onto their mothers as much as they can.

Some baby lemurs like to explore.

When the lemurs are five to six months old, they do not need their mothers anymore. They weigh almost 5 pounds (2 kilograms), or as much as a bag of sugar.

Lemurs are fully grown at one and a half years old.

A Good Meal

Until they are about six months old, young lemurs drink their mothers' milk. Then lemurs switch to a diet of solid foods.

Lemurs begin eating some solid foods at six weeks old. But they still need to nurse for about four more months.

Lemurs travel together from tree to tree looking for food.

The troop eats twice a day. They eat their first meal in the morning.

15

Babies learn from their mothers what foods are safe to eat.

Baby lemurs learn to eat by watching their mothers and the other lemurs. When a mother lemur eats some food, her baby will take a bite too.

After eating, the troop naps together in the trees. They wake up hungry. It is time to eat again!

Lemurs nap in a cozy pile.

Adult and baby lemurs mostly eat berries and other fruit.

Lemurs eat fruit, leaves, flowers, stems, and bark. Sometimes older lemurs catch small animals such as insects, chameleons, and birds.

Lemurs get water from the rain and morning dew. They lick the wet leaves of plants.

Lemurs might look for water in nearby rivers.

Growing Up

Lemurs play and wrestle together.

Lemurs are social animals. They spend time grooming one another. Lemurs also warm their bellies in the sun. At night, they sleep together in the trees.

Lemurs use their tails to communicate.

Ring-tailed lemurs often travel on the ground. They raise their tails in the air like flags. This helps lemurs see one another so they can stay together.

Troops must watch for predators such as hawks, buzzards, and fossas. When a lemur sees a predator, it makes a high-pitched sound to alert the others.

A lemur's loud warning keeps other lemurs safe.

Female lemurs stay with their group their whole lives, even after they become mothers.

A female lemur stays with the same troop its whole life. Male lemurs leave when they are about three years old. They join different troops during mating season.

Female lemurs mate when they are two or three years old. The males compete to mate with them.

A male and a female lemur perch together in a tree.

A male gets ready for a fight with another male.

Male lemurs fight one another. They rub their tails through stinky scent glands on their bodies and wave their tails over their heads. Then they stare at each other until one of them backs down.

Female lemurs usually have one baby each year. Orphans are adopted by other lemurs.

Both male and female ring-tailed lemurs can live to be twenty years old in the wild.

Lemur Life Cycle

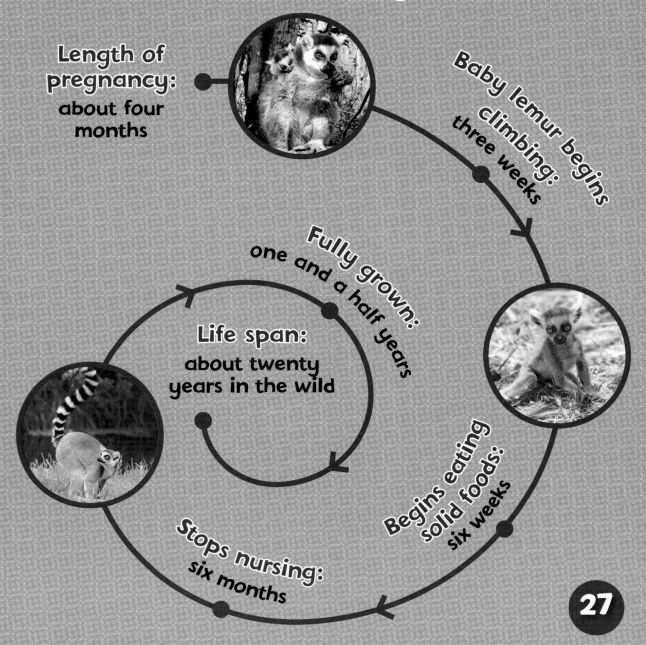

Length of pregnancy: about four months

Baby lemur begins climbing: three weeks

Fully grown: one and a half years

Life span: about twenty years in the wild

Begins eating solid foods: six weeks

Stops nursing: six months

Habitat in Focus

- Ring-tailed lemurs live in Madagascar, an island off the coast of Africa.

- During the rainy season, lemurs eat the fruit and leaves of Madagascar's tamarind trees. In the dry season, lemurs move around the island to find food.

- People are changing lemurs' habitat. Some people cut down tamarind trees to make room for farms. But other people are working to save Madagascar's forests.

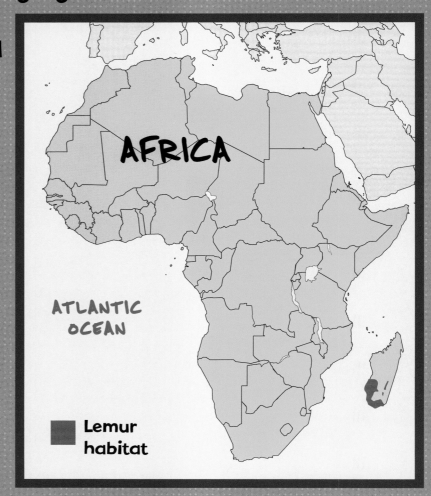

AFRICA

ATLANTIC OCEAN

■ Lemur habitat

Fun Facts

- A grown lemur's tail is about 2 feet (1 meter) long!

- There are usually thirteen rings on a lemur's tail.

- Ring-tailed lemurs make many different sounds. They purr, meow, howl, grunt, and bark.

- Lemurs have six bottom teeth that stick out. They use them like a comb.

Glossary

buzzard: a large bird that eats animals that are already dead

dew: water that collects on plants at night

fossa: a relative of the mongoose that lives only in the forests of Madagascar

groom: to clean an animal's fur and keep up its appearance

orphan: a baby animal whose parents have died

predator: an animal that kills and eats another animal

scent gland: a cell in the body that gives off a smell

Further Reading

DK. *Animals: A Visual Encyclopedia.* New York: DK, 2012.

Lemur Moms: National Aeronautics and Space Administration
http://climatekids.nasa.gov/lemurs

Oluonye, Mary N. *Madagascar.* Minneapolis: Lerner Publications, 2010.

Riley, Joelle. *Ring-Tailed Lemurs.* Minneapolis: Lerner Publications, 2009.

Ring-Tailed Lemur: Fort Wayne Children's Zoo
http://kidszoo.org/our-animals/central-zoo/ring-tailed-lemur

Ring-Tailed Lemurs: *National Geographic Kids*
http://kids.nationalgeographic.com/animals/ring-tailed-lemur

Spelman, Lucy. *Animal Encyclopedia.* Washington, DC: National Geographic, 2012.

Index

Photo Acknowledgments

The images in this book are used with the permission of: © Dennis van de Water/Shutterstock Images, pp. 2, 22; © Matejh photography/iStock/Thinkstock, p. 4; © dr322/Shutterstock Images, pp. 5, 27 (top); © nattanan726/Shutterstock Images, p. 6; © Pierre-Yves Babelon/Shutterstock Images, p. 7; © Steliost/Shutterstock Images, pp. 8, 27 (bottom right); © Henk Bentlage/Shutterstock Images, pp. 9, 11; © Micha/MyImages/Shutterstock Images, p. 10; © PAB Images/iStock/Thinkstock, p. 12; © wrangel/iStock/Thinkstock, pp. 13, 27 (bottom left); © Henk Bentlage/iStock/Thinkstock, pp. 14, 19; © Valentina Gabusi/iStock/Thinkstock, p. 15; © Eric Gevaert/Shutterstock Images, p. 16; © Paul Maguire/Shutterstock Images, pp. 17, 31; © Brian Gerber/iStock/Thinkstock, p. 18; © Dave M. Hunt Photography/Shutterstock Images, p. 20; © Roberto Caucino/Shutterstock Images, p. 21; © Age Fotostock Spain, S.L./Alamy, p. 23; © Fotomicar/Shutterstock Images, p. 24; © Chris Hellier/Alamy, p. 25; © tane mahuta/iStock/Thinkstock, p. 26; © NREY/Shutterstock Images, p. 30.

Cover Image: © Cyril Ruoso/Minden Pictures/Newscom

Main body text set in Johann light 30/36